EVERYTHING THE TORIES KNOW ABOUT COMPASSION

Gideon Cameron

CHAPTERS

Chapter ONE

Everything the Tories know about.... compassion

Fuck all.

Fuck All.

Fuck All.

Fuck All.

Fuck All.

Fuck All.

Fuck All.

Fuck All.

Fuck All.

Fuck All.

Fuck All.

Fuck All.

Fuck All.

Fuck All.

Chapter TWO

Everything the Tories know about.... Love

Fuck All.

Fuck All.

Fuck All.

Fuck All.

Fuck All.

Fuck All.

Fuck All.

Fuck All.

Fuck All.

Fuck All.

Fuck All.

Fuck All.

Fuck All.

Fuck All.

Fuck All.

Fuck All.

Fuck All.

Fuck All.

Fuck All.

Fuck All.

Fuck All.

Fuck All.

Fuck All.

Fuck All.

Fuck All.

Fuck All.

Fuck All.

Fuck All.

Fuck All.

Chapter THREE

Everything the Tories know about.... Empathy

Fuck All.

Fuck All.

Fuck All.

Fuck All.

Fuck All.

Fuck All.

Fuck All.

Fuck All.

Fuck All.

Fuck All.

Fuck All.

Fuck All.

Fuck All.

Fuck All.

Everything The Tories Know About Compassion

Fuck All.

Chapter FOUR

Everything the Tories know about.... Poverty

Fuck All.

Fuck All.

Fuck All.

Everything The Tories Know About Compassion

Fuck All.

Fuck All.

Fuck All.

Fuck All.

Fuck All.

Fuck All.

Fuck All.

Fuck All.

Fuck All.

Fuck All.

Fuck All.

Fuck All.

Chapter FIVE

Everything the Tories know about.... Fairness

Fuck All.

Fuck All.

Fuck All.

Fuck All.

Fuck All.

Fuck All.

Fuck All.

Fuck All.

Fuck All.

Fuck All.

Fuck All.

Fuck All.

Fuck All.

Fuck All.

Fuck All.

Fuck All.

Fuck All.

Fuck All.

Fuck All.

Fuck All.

Everything The Tories Know About Compassion

Fuck All.

Fuck All.

Fuck All.

Fuck All.

Fuck All.

Chapter SIX

Everything the Tories know about.... Helping those in need

Fuck All.

Fuck All.

Fuck All.

Fuck All.

Fuck All.

Fuck All.

Fuck All.

Fuck All.

Fuck All.

Fuck All.

Fuck All.

Fuck All.

Fuck All.

Fuck All.

Fuck All.

Fuck All.

Fuck All.

Fuck All.

Fuck All.Fuck All.

Fuck All.

Fuck All.

Fuck All.

Fuck All.

Fuck All.

Fuck All.

Fuck All.

Chapter SEVEN

Everything the Tories know about.... Culture

LOADS!

Only joking.

Fuck All.

Fuck All.

Fuck All.

Fuck All.

Fuck All.

Fuck All.

Fuck All.

Fuck All.

Fuck All.

Fuck All.

Fuck All.

Fuck All.

Fuck All.

Fuck All.

Fuck All.

Fuck All.

Fuck All.

Fuck All.

Fuck All.

Fuck All.

Chapter EIGHT

Everything the Tories know about.... Art

Fuck All.

Fuck All.

Fuck All.

Fuck All.

Fuck All.

Fuck All.

Fuck All.

Fuck All.

Fuck All.

Fuck All.

Fuck All.

Fuck All.

Fuck All.

Fuck All.

Everything The Tories Know About Compassion

Fuck All.

Fuck All.

Everything The Tories Know About Compassion

www.ingramcontent.com/pod-product-compliance
Lightning Source LLC
Chambersburg PA
CBHW020513290526
45786CB00002B/580